A Waterfall

An anthology of poetry with illustrative photographs

By

Meryl M Williams

Copyright © 2024 Meryl M Williams

All rights reserved, including the right to reproduce this book, or portions thereof in any form. No part of this text may be reproduced, transmitted, downloaded, decompiled, reverse engineered, or stored, in any form or introduced into any information storage and retrieval system, in any form or by any means, whether electronic or mechanical without the express written permission of the author.

The views expressed in this work are solely those of the author and do not necessarily reflect the views of the publisher, and the publisher hereby disclaims any responsibility for them.

ISBN: 978-1-917425-01-8

THE POET MERYL M WILLIAMS
b1966

Meryl was born in South Wales and trained originally in the biological sciences, studying in Cardiff then working in medical research in London, Bath and Texas USA. Since leaving science, she has settled in Bath writing first poetry then prose. Her work is inspired by faith, the appeal of the natural world and people she meets on her journey. She will write on subjects that are suggested to her also and has contributed to local newsletters.

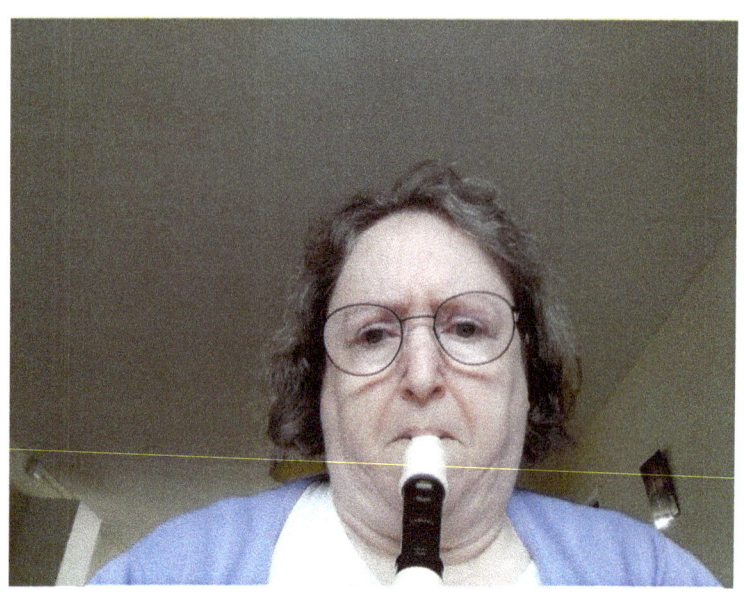

Other published works by the poet and author are:-

Moods in Bloom
The Judge Jones Trilogy
My Lady's Sovereign
Mortymer House-A Novella and
Treasure Within - A Memoir

UNATTAINABLE YOU

Beautiful! Beautiful! Beautiful love!
Repeat, repeat the ode.
Your body shines, your skin's aglow
For me you're never old.

Come back, come back, come back again
Restored and by my side,
I love far more than you can dream
My arms are open wide.

Lovely, darling, caring man
I'm with you evermore
We'll meet again, you'll wear your robe
For opening Abbey's door.

ENDEARING YOU

It is the modern way of life
A manly sport for women too
But we are most accepting here
Adapting with the times or price.

For Freedom is oft dearly won
The cup that slips, the flower fades
A cherished moment not repeated
A Spider's web of finest lace.

While winds blow in o'er land and sea
As showers burst yet sunrise beams
I will not ever leave your arms
This space, this place is meant to be.

But when I travel with my mind
I know you're never far away
For others inwardly are blind
But you could always, ever see.

The long awaited rains are here
All streaming, soaking, supped by earth
My soul rejoices for I feel
A good man, treasure trove can be.

WATER'S EDGE

Shimmering sunshine, golden stone
Light or shade of morning glow

Barges, locks and bridges built
Iron, steel, or stone would melt

Cast aside all care, all woe
Drown your worries here below

Find the surface of the Water
Lives with Nature's sons and daughters

Insects, spiders, life abundant
Floating humans, diving cormorant

Spread your wings howe'er you travel
Herons pause for all to marvel

While away this lovely morning
Carolling at every dawning

Then at dusk as wagtails play
Return again another day.

JAMBOREE

Colours bright, all blinding structure
Monkey wrench with stars appearing
Here's a pie chart made of wedges
This one is of tea cups cheering

I would love to try this art
Fabric made of tiny parts
Here is my design for you
Then I hope you'll see it through.

A team of stitchers do this justice
Impact holds for evermore
But I'll not forget the flip side
Every detail sewn galore

Here's my favourite, here's a quilt
I would dearly love to own
Sunrise in a million colours
Squares of light from outside in.

Penning this my chosen craft
I pay tribute to his art
For each circle is enduring
Surrounded by a square of winning.

THE WATERMILL AT BATHAMPTON

It was said the wheel
Turned the restaurant floor
But at high water spun too fast
Rivers wax or wane with rains
A Weir floods like never before

Gentle movement encapsulated
By a piece of soothing music
Composed and used for 'Secret Garden'
Memory of a cherished father

Elizabethan serenade
Sings of sunshine through the age
For a Princess, then a Queen
Now at peace, so all serene
At an everlasting place
Holy, worthy, end of race

But beginnings start at ends
Here the future love will send
Gracious mama smiling down
Generations of successions
Dine here at the water's edge.

SHEPHERDS WALK

A pretty footpath through woods we wend
Has wildflowers, birdsong, pheasant calls,
A cuckoo in spring.

Nettle is loved by butterflies
Here it's creamy, almost yellow flowers
Curl to encourage pollinators
To dip for nectar within.

The nettle leaves are green all year
Also adored by wasps that abound
Plus tiny black and yellow hover flies
As Nature often repeats herself
Warning that these critters are not good to eat
While bees are buzzing close to the ground.

For to many insects, that creep or crawl
It's the dead nettle that's found to be good as a feast.

OUR PHILOSOPHY

Why is a blackberry?
It clutters up the hedgerows
Must be cleared from my garden
But encourages birds and bees to feast
A shiny, tasty, morsel, good to eat.

Sharp but tangy, lay them on a plate
Let the crawling creatures leave
Bake with apples, crumbles, pies
Divine, devoured, why not a blackberry?

Why are the larvae?
Well Nature is full of fat and fed
The fly reposes on a flower
But when I come back he's moved
To feed amongst all things nectar

Why write this poem?
I think therefore I am!

SHAM CASTLE

High upon a hilltop
Overlooking Bath
Here's a fairy's homestead
Built just for a laugh!

Just a wall of honeyed stone
Turrets either side
Behind there's nothing
But fresh air, the grass
The fields, all wild.

Providing us this viewpoint
Observed from down below
No charge to see around it
It was only built for show.

Does this not provide us
With a timed analogy?
Vanity surrounds us
With false posterity!

A PERFECT IDEAL

Born of man, divinely made
Knit from all things ethereal,
Aspire, go higher, leave behind,
Dross worldly pleasures, be pure of mind
Cast aside the weight of sin
See the depth of love within
This is all you'll ever need
Rest, at peace, His grace is here.
Just consider earthly view, Nature's wonder
Some man made, pause in awe
It's splendour gazing
Distant haze with nearby grazing,
Lord how thankful now I am
For the sense to carry on
Praising you in every way
This, my living, loving day.

WINTER VIEW

Here I take a timely snap
Bare the branches, cold the sky
Suddenly I see between
All that I had lost to view.

Far away horizons calling
Distant hills so lost and lonesome
For to travel is my aim
As my footsteps itch to claim
Terra Firma, miles of roaming
Yet I stand, I'm going nowhere.

Time stands still as trees resilient
Bend or break to winds insistence
Oh for chance to blow away
Leave forever, lose the day
Embrace the opportunity
Get out now, without regret
Don't look back, the stage is set.

SUMMER AT THE FIRS

See the dog owners with their pets
Walks for daily discipline,
Here I am to enjoy fresh air
Picnics pleasure on this seat.

A spider joined my solitary feast
I gazed in wonder at this extraordinary beast
Yellow stripes adorned her body
Her web she wove with dogged determination
Showing such committed patience.

Entangled as the ties of love
From the ethos all above
All around us and below
Yet the muse he didn't show
But that's ok, I'll get him back
With Nature's inspiration
And a touch of divination
The poem surely followed
A snap to catch this moment.

HIDDEN MYSTERIES

A cherub resides, entombed in stone
Buried, forgotten, re-born
I heard it came from happier times
Petrified yet adorning the stone

Face down in the dust
Who knew it was there?
It's story or legacy lost
What inscription did it bear?

Did the deceased have lands or largesse?
Was this memorial at terrible cost?
Perhaps we will not encounter
Remains to establish a pointer
Leading to our understanding
Of why a cherub, attached to a pillar
Should now in stone be silent
As the grave.

But if we should discover how
It's owners lived and died
The story must ever survive.

UNDER A DESERT SKY

Lapis lazuli desert sky
Cold nights, searing days
Sand, rock, barren tree
Satan as a hornet
Persistent will ever be.

Forty days and nights of fasting
Now the wasp presents a stone
Turn this into bread he taunts thus
But no, we need not bread alone
Every word from God is honoured
For a life of goodly tone.

Now the fiend suggests a test
Cast yourself upon these stones
But the Lord rebuked this spirit
Do not test thy God at all.

Finally as Satan endures
Offerings of kingdoms, palaces
All that was not his
Jesus spoke to affirm his calling
Worship one God alone, never the fallen.

Angels came to tend the Lord
Satan found a dwelling place
In the heart of willing Judas
Born to sell the soul of fate.

LANDSCAPES IN WORDS

Natural features enfold a symbol of man's creation
Working together harmoniously
Controlling a force of elevation.

Seemingly defiant of law of gravitation
Water carries stone above the valley
Left by water or hewn with shovel
Rail, river, road parallel to each other.

Trees are bare, the hedgerows scruffy
Ferns nestle in evergreen splendour
See the lapis lazuli sky
Blue as lit by Heaven's wonder.

Blaze the sunshine, yet chill the wind
Narrow boats with cheerful colours
Everyone a happy name, logs of wood
For stoves to heat the same.

Here I find such perfect peace
Bliss to encounter sweet release.

STORM CLOUDS

Thunderous the skies are seeming
Summer's morning, waters greeting
This the time I saw you last
Hold our distant memories fast
Lake of grey with life abundant
Moorhens, coots, as gulls triumphant
Feed or forage while they may
Live to breed another day
We are happy just to linger
Views inspiring, awesome hunger
Poet's quest to be redeemed
By this lovely, lonely world.
For if God indeed exists
Find him at a place like this
Rejoice in all his majesty
Thanks Welsh water
Now for tea!

RON

The darkest night is all aflame
With my memories of your name
We may now be always parted
But here's to musings open hearted.

First I loved your kindly face
Winning, smiling, shining grace
Then we met to help each other
At a shared and good endeavour.

In my life I had a dream
To draw your hands from love extreme
Such a character shown with pencil
Marked upon my heart as a stencil
Just a fervent memory now
But my dear I am so proud.

Coffee mornings dined Al fresco
You were happy, I am glad
Looking back at what we had
Such a worthy practice for you
I'm so blessed to know I met you.

UNSUITED

A Grandfather much less formal
With open necked shirt
Topped by a warm pullover

Describing Devon not Cornish pasties
Happy days at men's cricket
Decorating a much loved church for Christmas
All down at Epiphany
Like the clack of wickets falling

Every year in endless cycling
But different each time
Such a long held mystery
All unseen with quiet privacy.

DAVID

This your endeavour to last forever
Built of glass with stone
Suited, robed at the front door
A smile to melt the poles.

Such a caring, listening wisdom
I remember you today
For support so kindly dealt with
Will never go away.

With the angels, truly blessed
You are Kith and kin
Playing at toy soldiers sometime
Joy of glow within.

I am hoping I will meet you
More than once again
At the heavenly righteous feasting
Banquet for us all redeeming
At the end of time.

RODNEY

A spark lights up a thousand bulbs
Electricity adorns your very personality
Manly your stride along the Side Aisle
Perfect your form, suited with
Embroidered waistcoat, I bought you a tie
It was yellow for Easter.

We enjoyed all things and
Renovated your escritoire
At the craft festival.

Sweet the kiss, so ethereal
Firm the hug, all warm and near
Then your service to the church
Could only end with your demise.

Devotion, duty, a certain calling
All things spiritual, materials forming
See the sword, the gauntlet as
Exhibits with our late view of
Magna Carta 1215 so now
Hereafter, you have said
Your ashes to be scattered are
Such that none on earth shall stay.

BLACK AND WHITE

Uniform pressed as precise as a pin
Black trews, white shirt, black tie
Seemingly no turmoil within

But life is not encapsulated
With such sharp boundaries
Between a well defined imagination
No, all is not the calm it seems

You lock the doors at night
Then reopen if we're lucky
But then with Christmas comes a lovely song
That pens in music what I dream

For you my enemy are my friend
The gate is open, here I leave
It's kind of you to wish me well

With smiling face it's 'all the best'
Do not not ever come again
I didn't but I thank you because
A new era has finally dawned.

PRETTY IN PINK

Sumptuous fabric of satin in pink
To make a project, an applique quilt

Scallop shells with demarkation
Green for the edges, a fertile imagination

Dancing ladies, dark haired girls
Red bows in their hair

A lord a leaping floats above
He's dressed like Hamlet here

While sundry jewels of fabric made
Surround the maverick dancers staid

Then for the flip side, dusky pink
As quilting will adorn I think
To finish off the whole.

MONOPOLISING THE MINISTER

Hear words of wisdom
From a priest a while ago
Depart in Joy by preference
I just wish to say Goodbye

Some have a range of issues
While many make complaint
I'd never dare to interrupt
I simply pause to wait

I'm not remotely saintly
Nor preachy perfect yet
I presume your needs are pressing
I'll pass by and save the rest.

Another day is dawning
Always a second chance
There's letter, 'phone or email
Next week or sometime hence.

I find a queue so awkward
But unless it must be said
I'll sleep on that same issue
Then pen my art instead.

RETALIATION

When I a young school student was
Some boys were rather rough
And from the stairwell they would spit
Just thinking they were tough

I spoke with my school teacher
As he was heard to ask
"What would they do where you're from?"
Of a visitor from France.

"We'd sort it out between us",
This the considered reply
"We'd not involve the teacher".
So my friend had this to say.

"You spat on me! Punch!" She suggested
Was the start of fights and war
A vigilante tactic
That ends with death and more.

Her wisdom comes back to me
As war rants on and on
It's miles away, we have no say
While peoples suffer endlessly
In total, sheer futility
So here we tighten up our belts
Claiming we live in poverty
We have no clue at all.

Sharon if you read my book
To you goes out this call
Always turn the other cheek
Or the weakest go to the wall.

THE EMPIRE HOTEL

A landmark worthy of the name
This famous building towers above
A pretty municipal park.

It's skyline shows all classes of people
Were represented in its heyday
A castle, a manor, a cottage.

These days it's transformed
Into special apartments
With a restaurant beneath.

Tourists who see this sight today
May overlook The Empire per se
As they visit the gardens or Abbey nearby.

Residents speak of revellers at night
But what a pretty view to sight
A landmark indeed, convenient to live

While the River Avon flows
Oblivious of all our woes
Home to boaters with birds and fish in their droves.

Inspirational is the thought
It was inclusive before the War
Then an office for the Admiralty
Now full of comforts with every luxury.

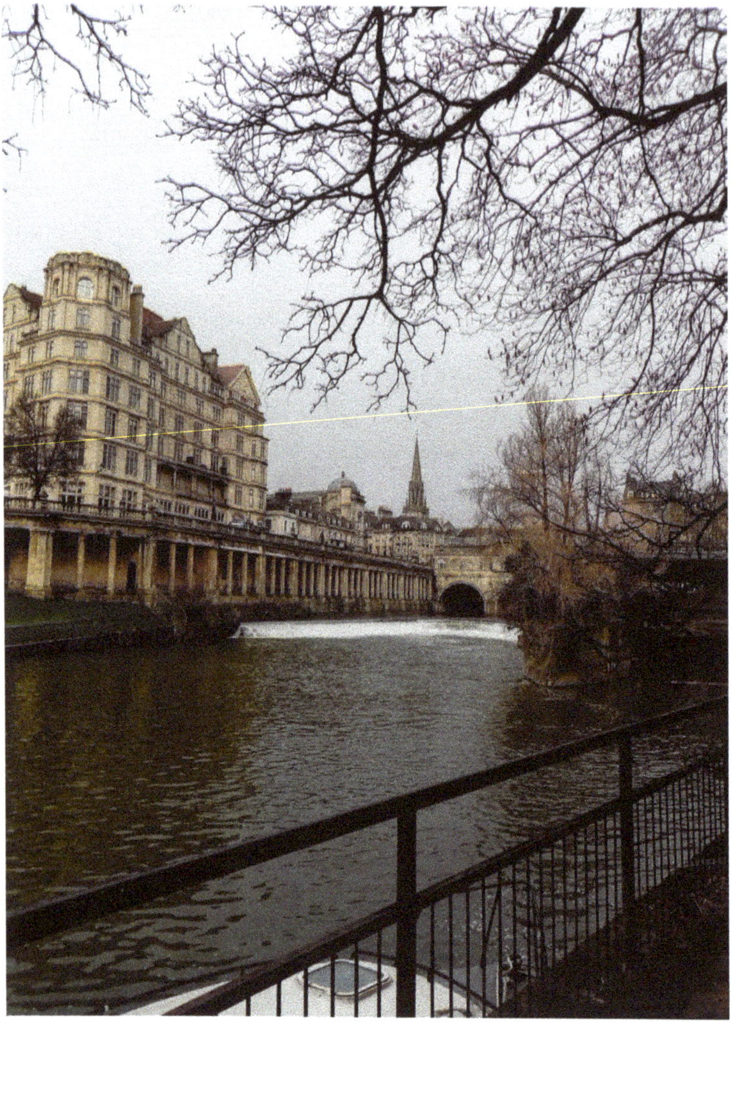

SUMMER SUNSHINE COLOUR

Poppies bedeck the highways bold
A cheering, heaven sent sight to behold
Single or double, yellow or red
Long stemmed, lovely
Yet scentless it's said.

Pink or even burgundy
Cultivated, scattered, leaves of green
Bring a taste of longer days
Warmer nights and distant haze
Best left growing, prolong their stay
Leave to enjoy for all to see.

Red reminds us of a war
When poppies grew amongst dead by score
But all of that is yesteryear
I just am amazed at the colours galore.

No pigment made by mere mortal
Can match the hand of God's Creation
The joy these lovely flowers bring
Enlivens every living thing.

Some love the roses, some our trees
Many adore spring, others love the Fall
But pretty as a poppy is
It's bloom will fade as shall we all
So as there is but one chance only
I snapped this shot worth more than money.

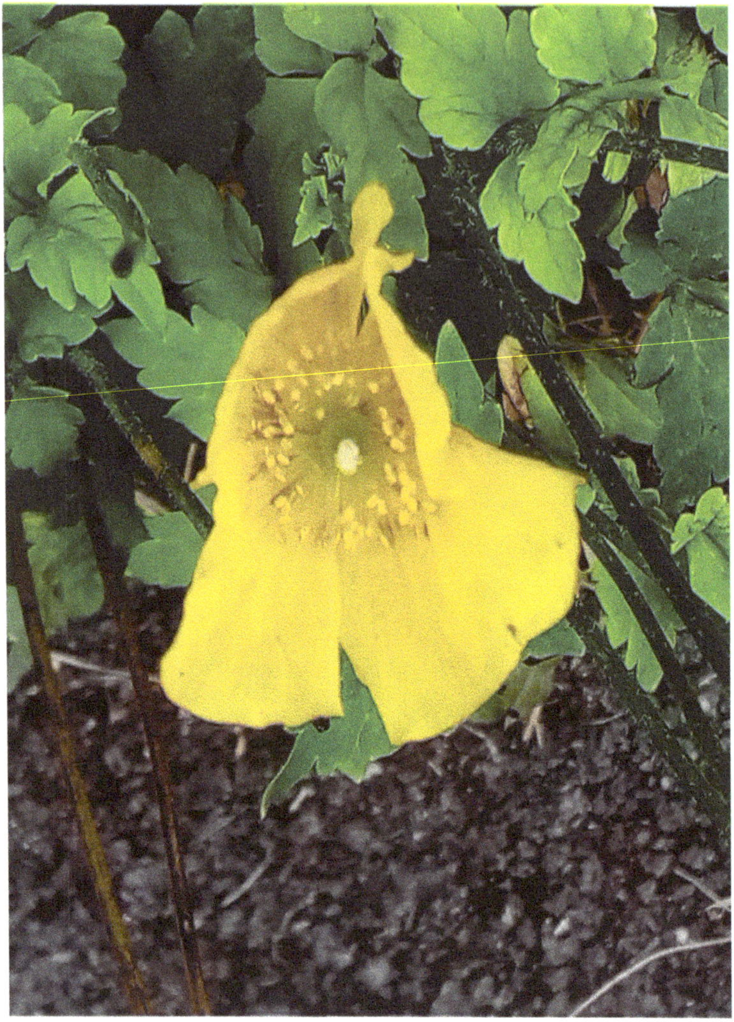

LARGER THAN LIFE

I walked the whole of Bath's Two Tunnels
So pleased the lights were on so bright
No daylight yet as such a curve
Hid the end from view, I persevered
Filled with wonder at the engineering
The brick with natural rock
Blasted by dynamite, celebrated
In literature later created.

The second tunnel lasts a mile
It's under Combe Down hill
Emerging there a road that led
To church at Monkton Combe
An iconic viewpoint, here you see
Modern express trains on a viaduct
Still in use today.

A Macro shot is larger than life
So these stones look super huge
Reminding me of long, tidy path
Through those tunnels away from traffic
With a bench to recognize Bath heroes
As an escapism to the countryside
With a lovely Manor House
All overlooking where I reside.

I must be honest, it took nerves of steel
I didn't dare look back
A route to my left at Tucking Mill

A lake, a cottage, tall trees, then a signpost
Bringing much relief.

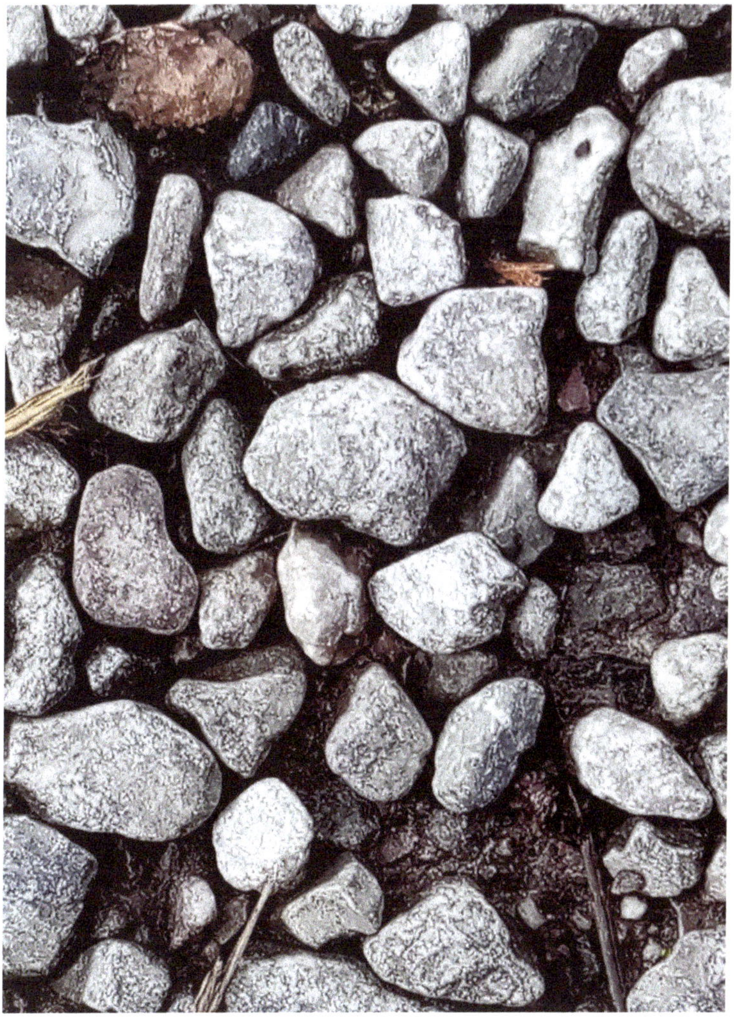

FEASTING BEAST

Aphids, green fly, all good food
This ladybug is surrounded
A red creature, black spots
Munching while I capture
It's a completely satisfying rapture.

Moments caught on camera can
Behold a glimpse of time
A fleeting second, ne're returned
Just a bug eating, as I am contemplating
It's peaceful, serene, mindful, truly
Absorbing state of mind.

Nearby, a wasp was feeding too
This patch of wildflowers growing through
Right next a High Street full of people
Cars for business, throbbing hub
Chairs outside a local pub

The contrast strikes my thoughtful nature
A tribute to the Friends of Widcombe
Such an oasis in the city
Green, alive, so very pretty
A lung for all to see
A space for all to breathe.

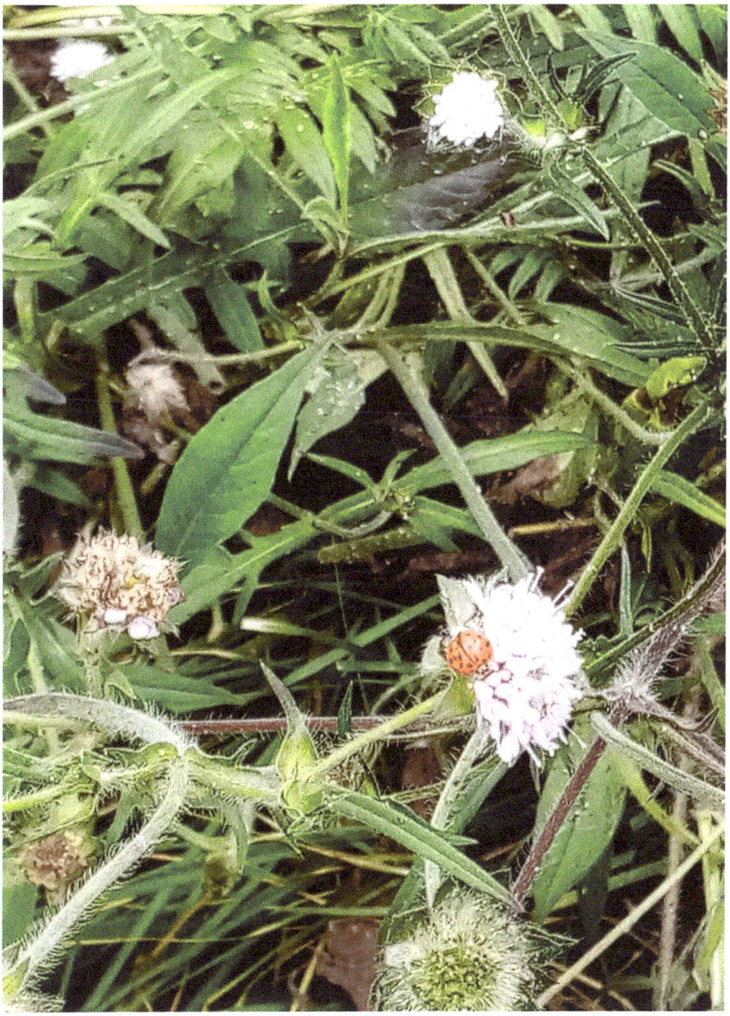

WELSH SLATE

A crazy paving wrought, in blocks of fine Welsh slate
Designed like natural currency, all dark grey and beautifully inlaid.

The cross cut shows the grain, reminding me of coasters for sale
In curiosity shops where squirrels, birds or landmarks are engraved

Industry marches on, inexorable the change of time
But this wonderful, natural stone, breathes long of lost aeons.

In a circle the blocks of slate are designed,
Quarried once, where tourists now beat the paths
Wearing down ancient hillsides, as humankind makes its marks.

Opposite the slate, in the gallery as dominates a wall
An intriguing image of a graveyard, rich with grass
Some weeds, many tombstones, but how to make sense of it all?

An evocative time spent here, an endeavour rewarded with joy
Outside the sun is shining while Bristol Crown looks
Deceptively silent from a safe distance, on this lovely Sunday in July.

ON CONSTABLE

Such a visual, unbelievable creation of art
See the detail of even the tracks left by the cart

A dog, the riverbank, black horses, trappings complete
A huge edifice, six foot wide, as large as life in effect

Awe I feel to think that this has been painted
With water like burnished steel, or glass here created

Reflections as in a photograph, yet more alive, with the hay wain made of wood
Contemplated by a drover as he stood, peaceful, serene in his smock
Speaking of yesteryear, but herein lies a tale

The riverbanks are steep on either side, so how does the drover drive?
To take his empty cart forward or back, no he is forever in this river
Encapsulated in art.

SUNDAY BRASS

Newly refurbished, roses around the edge
A band stand built with iron musical notes
Decorating its railings, a roof but no walls.

A band set up their gleaming brass
Then waited under a tree for the cue to start
Orderly the discipline of sitting and standing
All at their desks, a musical term for music stands.

Sounds floated o'er the parkside waters
Children dance from deckchairs nearby
Change since my childhood - many ladies in the band.

My neighbour on this wooden seat
Films the action on handheld phone
The whole conducted by a waistcoated man
Songs old and new, what sweet relaxation
For a Sunday afternoon.

SURROUNDINGS

It's said a camera never lies
Look left to view this dome
It is an ancient building
Where the municipal library
Once had its home.

Now it houses art
Currently posters of Montmartre
With a wonderful Thomas Gainsborough
Who showed a deep reluctance
For painting his subject's hands.

See how the costume of his day
Is beautifully portrayed
The longer, brightly coloured dress coat
Pantaloons, stockings, buckled shoes
All elegantly displayed.

The child also a vision
Amazingly like his Dad
While all the time
A dog looks on
Creations brought to life.

Looking again at my photograph
It's all sliding toward the river
While catacombs are underneath
Rumoured to make a Cellar Bar.

Pulteney Bridge has businesses
Plus a very shabby rear view
The whole seen from a pleasure cruise
An ancient pastime too.

Our River Avon looks today
Deceptively calm for sport or play
Thank you boatmen, it was super
There was a heron and it
Was well worth doing.

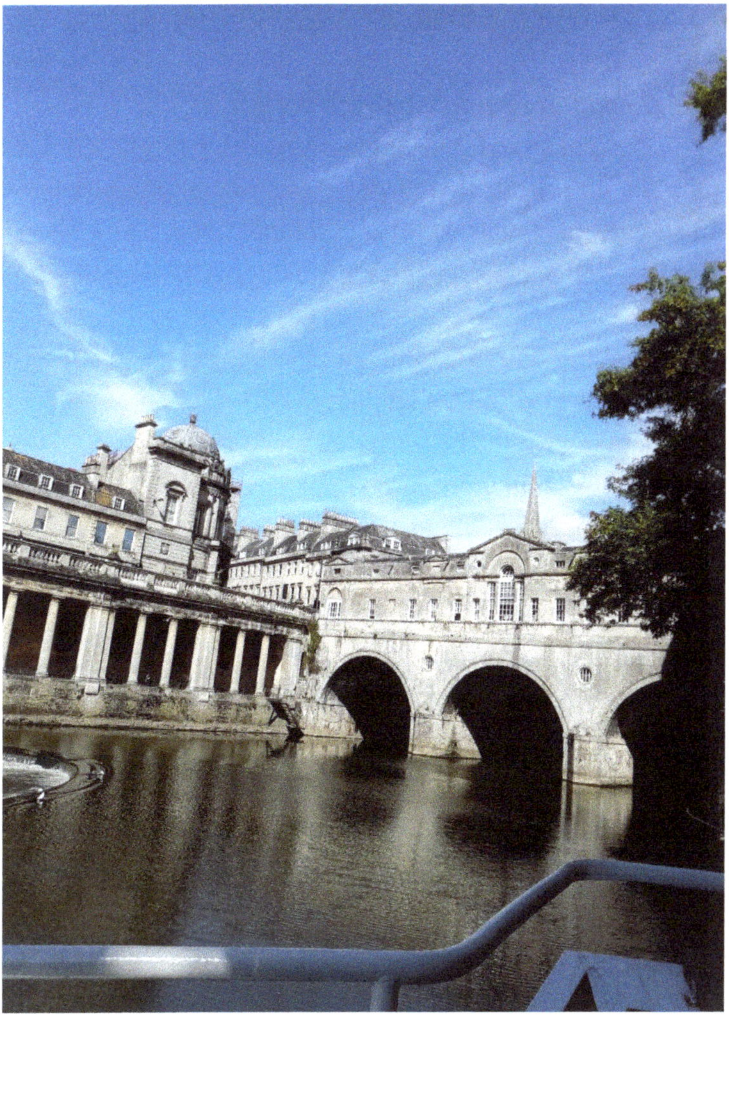

CLAVERTON MANOR

Dallas and I discovered this, our perfect spot
With stunning views, so English yet
Our history revealed within
Lush gardens, lawns, shrubs, parkland, trees
Topiary immaculate, coach house, buggy, all complete.

I descend the staircase, grand and sweeping
Behold a harp, a flute, a spinnet
A canopy above the bed
Silk fittings, mother of pearl
Silver, gold, riches inlaid

But now a Museum preserved it is,
With a team of ardent enthusiasts,
Such loving care, enjoyment here
A place to return to every year,
Then back outside to admire those views
I'm here once more, a Frank is called for!

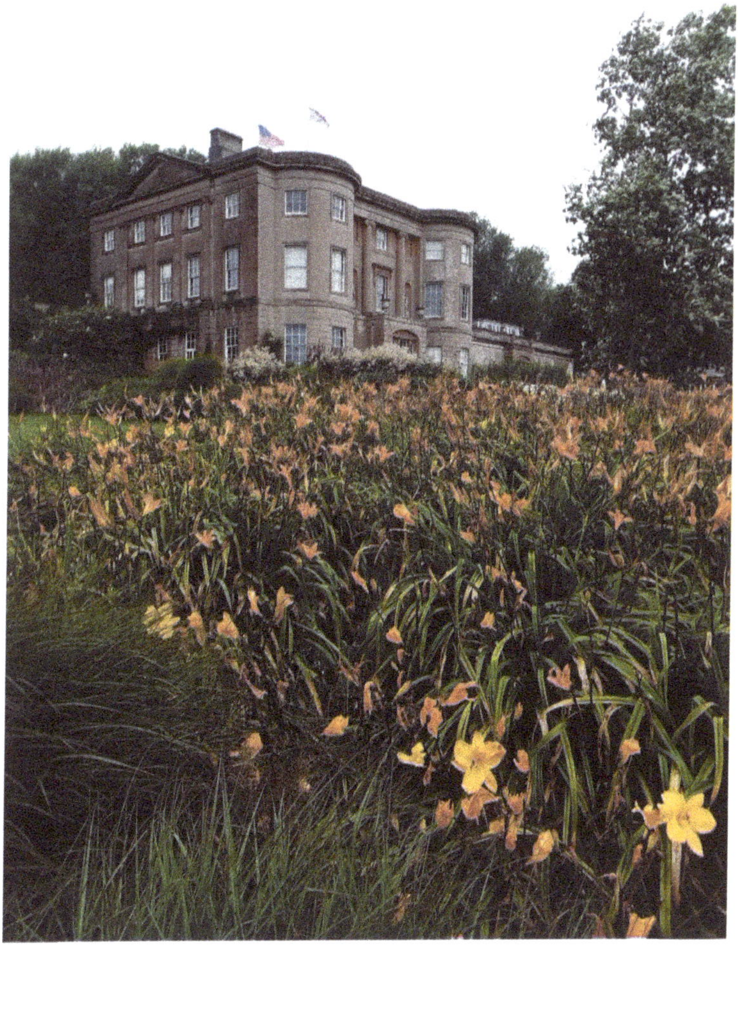

HENRIETTA PARK

All around the oblong pond
Is a wooden pergola, wreathed in a climbing rose
Stems, wooden, knotted, twisted, aged
But lovely flowers in two tone
As if from a single plant
Orange and cream by nature's perfect, faultless art.

Every petal embraces its own
Some are overblown
Centred where the bees have been
Are stamens of brown, promising fruit
Rose hips come with autumn mists
Red, said to be full of vitamin C!

This secret garden in the city
Is a joy to behold, immeasurably pretty
While all around Bath denizens
Dog walking is enjoyed by fellow citizens
But words are insufficient
To pen the emotion but the camera
Captures a still to show in colour
With cultivation, what we can give to each other.

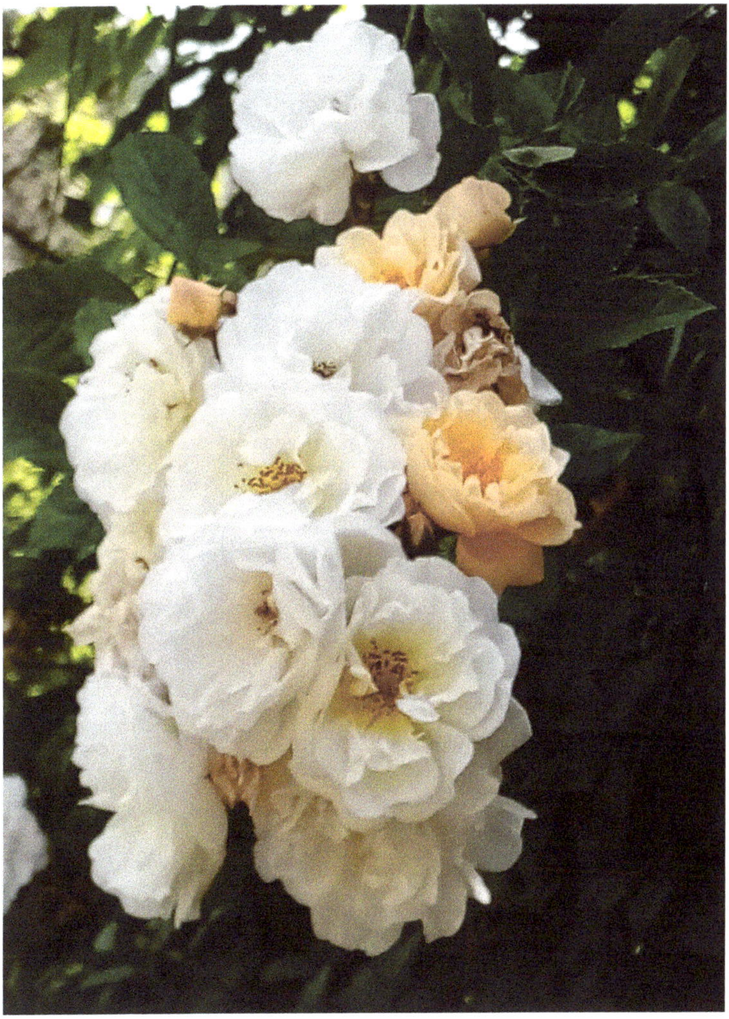

A BLANK CANVAS

Although a modern biro is not a quill
An empty page beguiles me
My spectacles rest as I compose
Thoughts busy with objects beside me.

I spent a fabulous afternoon
At a local gallery for arts
Admiring bronze, stone, plaster
All in miniature with perfect articulation
I'm lost in wonder, awe and adulation.

Here, the amazing Henry Moore
Had crafted around a Scallop shell
To give the mother a full, long skirt
There was a display of his materials
So here in detail are mine.

A pen, a page, my spectacles
Ready for my art
To write a tiny tribute in miniature
For a genius who passed
In my final year of College
And whose sculpture I can see from a Thames boat.

If anything needed to be explained
Each caption gives such insight
I never realised before
My local gallery opened this door
Into a new world of wonder, delight, inspiration and awe.

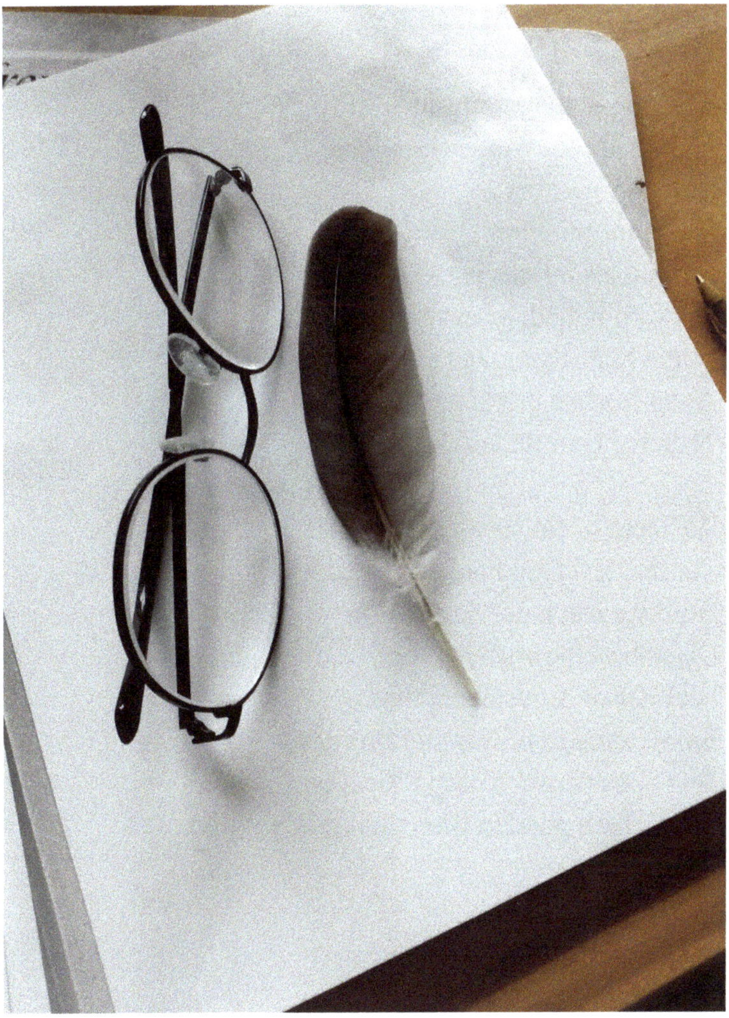

CASCADING CADENCE

A waterfall makes music
Too lovely for words
Rushing, gushing
Each murmuration
Of bubbles unceasing
Seaward bound, a heavenly sound.
While high above, the gulls are soaring
As spirits rise this sunny morning
Then the boat turns around.

We learn of flood, we see the skiffs
Those Cleveland Pools deserted lie,
Until we reach our destination
Disembarking with joy for life.
Feelings of refreshment thus,
Enjoy remains of this glorious day
And consider with deep reflection
Of all that's good in life's direction.

PARASITE OR SAPROPHYTE?

Allegedly this fungus, found on a fallen log
Is a Smoky Polypore, such fascinating
Folds of flesh, which I do not dream to disturb.

It's a parasite feeding greedily from
The phloem of the tree on which it feeds
Then I am reminded of a bus trip
Along a motor way, where huge oak trees
Line the route, full of great, fat bundles
Of Mistletoe that is entwined.

This greenery plucked for Christmas
With berries milky white
Gives something back to its partner Oak
So is a saprophyte.

Just view those amazing clusters
As Druids once foretold
While back home, the fallen tree trunk
Has Polypore in its folds.

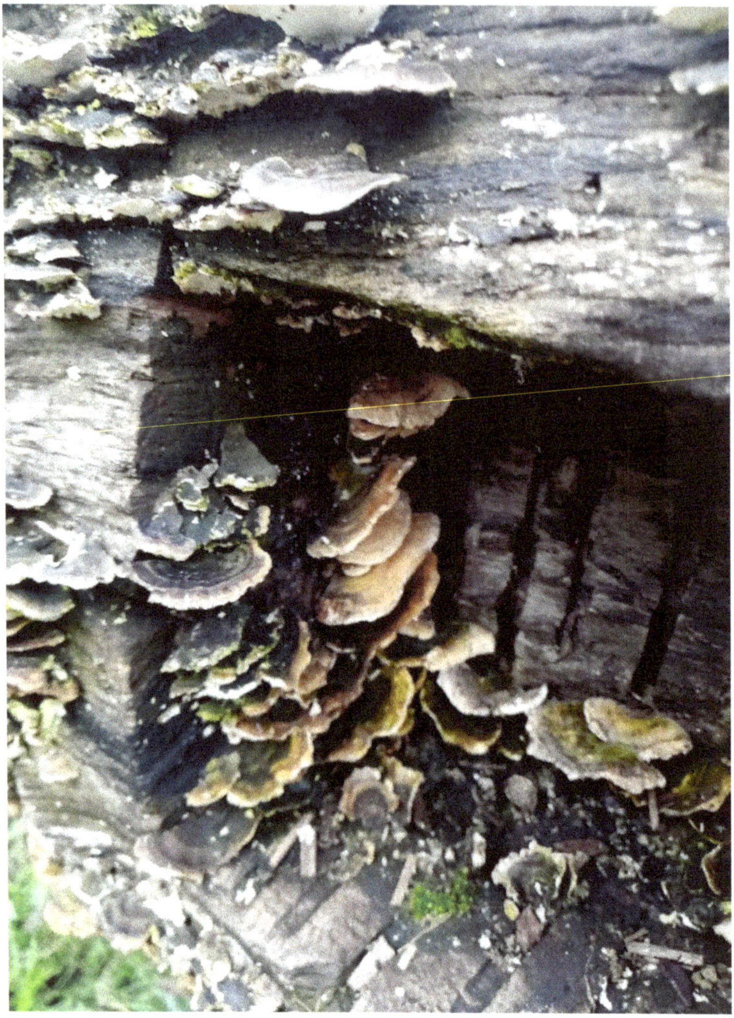

AN HOUR AWAY

Gloucester Historic Docks
Where yachts and barges mingle
The Canals Museum fascinates
With Folk Art of roses, bridges
Horse buckets, canalside scenes
Overlooked by waterfront business
Of every type from Sharpness to Severn River.

Inside an ancient warehouse,
From a long lost, bygone era
A model of a tall ship
To demonstrate its construction
By folk who lived by the Weir.

Looking over the whole display
From the city centre not far away
Stands in grey stone the Cathedral Tower
Built of clean lines with carved pinnacles
Surrounded by a fine piazza
Rest for the weary, calm, quiet, peace

Then my steps onward take me
To the Community Library
Where I visit today
Leaving my books at this
Lovely tranquil location
May it forever stay.

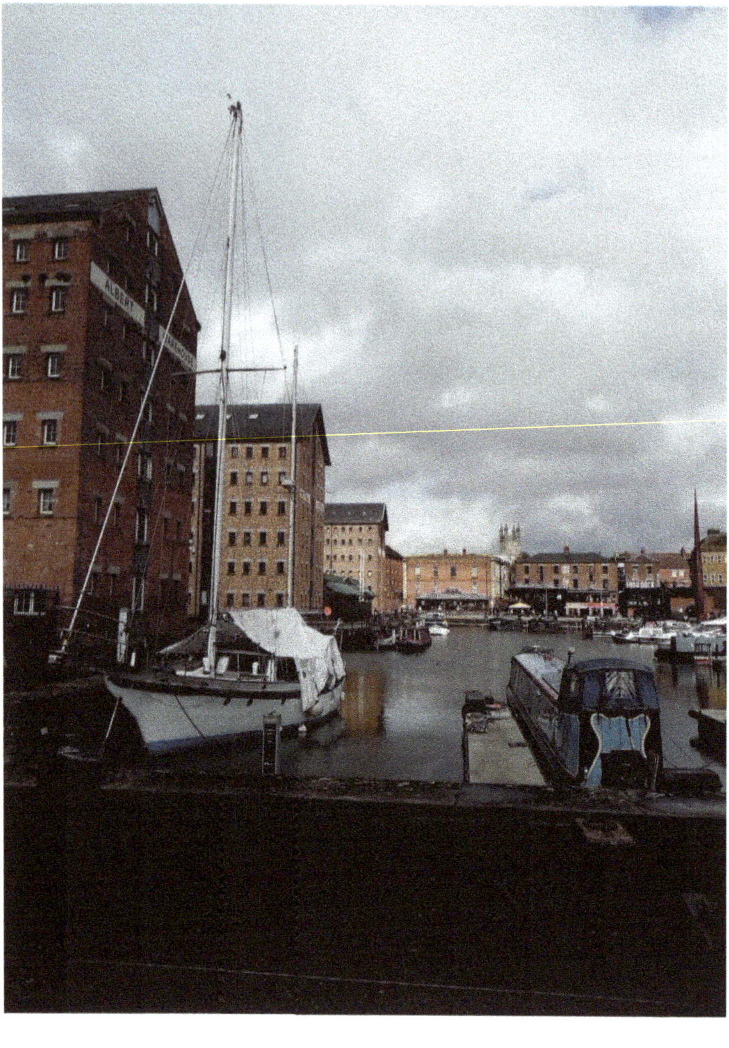
ALBERT

Index of first lines

Page no.
A cherub resides in stone.
22
A crazy paving wrought, in blocks of fine Welsh slate.
48
A Grandfather much less formal.
30
A landmark worthy of the name.
39
A pretty footpath through woods we wend.
10
A spark lights up a thousand bulbs.
33
A waterfall makes music.
60
All around the oblong pond.
56
Allegedly this fungus, found on a fallen log.
61
Although a modern biro is not a quill.
58
Aphids, green fly, all good food.
46
Beautiful! Beautiful! Beautiful love!
1
Born of man, divinely made.
16

Colours bright, all blinding structure.
6
Dallas and I discovered this, our perfect spot.
54
Gloucester Historic Docks.
63
Hear words of wisdom.
36
Here I take a timely snap.
18
High upon a hilltop.
14
I walked the whole of Bath's Two Tunnels.
43
It is the modern way of life.
2
It was said, the wheel.
8
It's said the camera never lies.
51
Lapis lazuli desert sky.
24
Natural features enfold a symbol of man's creation.
26
Newly refurbished, roses around the edge.
50
Poppies bedeck the highways bold.
41
See the dog owners with their pets.
20

Shimmering sunshine, golden stone.
4
Such a visual, unbelievable creation of art.
49
Sumptuous fabric of satin pink
35
The darkest night is all aflame.
30
This, your endeavour to last forever.
31
Thunderous the skies are seeming.
28
Uniform pressed as precise as a pin.
34
When I a young school student was.
37
Why is a blackberry?
12

Milton Keynes UK
Ingram Content Group UK Ltd.
UKHW021600230824
447235UK00007B/277